How to Create Your

www.AllWriteInk.com

www.TheSocialMediaRoadmap.com

Deborah Chaddock Brown

©January 2015

118 W. Streetsboro, Suite 144

Hudson, OH 44236

330-414-8792 Deborah@allwriteink.com

ISBN-13: 978-1505888232

ISBN -10: 1505888239

How to Create a Social Media Roadmap

Social Media is all over the news. We can't escape it. We may try to put our heads in the sand but while we are ducking reality our competition is storming the gates.

Consumers are already immersed in YouTube, Facebook and Twitter while recruiters, business leaders and marketers are hooked on the business connections LinkedIn provide.

Before you decide that you still aren't ready to incorporate social media into your marketing plan, consider these statistics published by the Huffington Post at the beginning of 2013:

- **1 Million** websites have integrated with **Facebook**
- **23%** of users check **Facebook 5 times** or more daily
- **56%** of customer **tweets** are being ignored
- **34%** of marketers have generated leads on **Twitter**
- **Google's +1** button is used **5 million times** a day
- Over **5 million photos** are uploaded to **Instagram every hour**

Let's not forget **LinkedIn** – the number one business networking site in the world. At a recent presentation the CEO of LinkedIn, Jeff Weiner, offered these numbers:

- Over 240 Million members, growing at 2 members per second.
- Adding 50 million members in the last year alone. It took 6 years to add their first 50 million members.
- LinkedIn just hit 10 million members from Brazil, which makes it the third largest country on LinkedIn along with the UK, behind the US and India.
- LinkedIn expects to reach 5 billion professional searches this year alone.
- Over 1 million groups have been created that contain between 2 and quarter of a million members.

Now that we have established that social media isn't just a passing phase, let's consider how we can harness the power and the numbers for YOUR business.

Deborah here...

You may not be ready to fully immerse your business into social media but being forewarned is forearmed. This workbook will help you understand the process of creating a roadmap for your Internet presence. Throughout this workbook I will share a tip or a word of encouragement, a "Dose of Deborah." Hang in there! I know you are going to be successful.

How to Create a Social Media Roadmap

In the following pages, we will walk through a process that starts with your goals and target audience and ends with a specific, task-oriented, customized plan for your social media participation.

Although there are over 550 social media networks on the Internet (and growing by the day) you only have to be present, participative and proactive on a few to successfully connect with your target audience.

Best of luck in the development of your Social Media Roadmap and contact me if you have questions, comments or stories to share!

Left blank for your notes

Table of Contents

Section One: Determining the Right R.O.A.D..........................7

- **R**esults
- **O**riginality
- **A**udience
- **D**irection

Section Two: Examining Different Paths for Your Roadmap.....15

- **Basics: Be An Option...17**
    - Your website
    - Email marketing
    - Online directories
    - Press Releases
- **The SOCIAL Part of The Roadmap...26**
- Casual Communicator...27
    - Facebook
    - Tumblr
- Professional Networker...32
    - LinkedIn
    - Google+
    - Blog
- Visual Spirit...49
    - Pinterest
    - YouTube
    - Meme
    - QR Tags
- Instantaneous Sharer..58
    - Twitter
    - Instagram

Section Three: Creating Your Social Media Roadmap..................65

- Narrow the field:
    - Must Have NOW
    - Short Term Goals
    - Long Term Goals
- Time Commitment: Daily/Weekly/Monthly
- Resources Needed
- Corporate Voice

Social Media Roadmap Worksheets..70

Quick Summary..72

Final Thoughts...74

About the Author..76

SECTION ONE: Determining the Right R.O.A.D.

R: Results – what result to do you hope to achieve with social media?

- Build customer relationships
- Create brand awareness
- Drive traffic to your website
- Improve your organic search results

As you begin the process you might be tempted to say that your goal is all four of the above reasons for participating in social media.

However, in order to be focused, you must select on primary goal. The reality is all roads lead to the same place; some are just more direct than others. Let's be honest and name our *real* goal.

The result I desire is to make money.

Does that sound about right? Although that may truly be our end game, without paying customers, we will be hard pressed to achieve it. Thus the need for a two-way conversation that social media can provide.

So let's examine those four goals a little closer:

Build customer relationships.

Social media allows us the opportunity to ask questions, listen to concerns and follow discussions that reveal the expectations and needs of our customers. Just like in the physical world, it takes time to build relationships with social media. However, the community that you develop will be interactive, supportive, encouraging and loyal.

Create brand awareness.

Perhaps you need to put the horse before the cart; do people even know your business exists? Maybe you would prefer spending time creating content with your company name, products and services and sharing your knowledge. This is more of a one way conversation but can certainly benefit your business in the long run by keeping your name in front of prospects. Eventually they will have a need of your products and/or services and if you have been diligent with brand awareness, they will remember your name.

Drive traffic to your website.

Does your website tell the whole story? Is your business such that all the consumer needs to do is find your site and the rest will take care of itself? There is a business called Poo-Pourri (http://www.poopourri.com/) that sells spray scents that contain body fluid odors to the toilet bowl. The story is funny and yet rings a bell of truth. I challenge you to visit their site and not make a purchase!

Improve organic search results.

In other words, land on the first page of the search results. With Google's ever changing method of indexing web pages, this is a moving target, but some social media sites help this goal better than others.

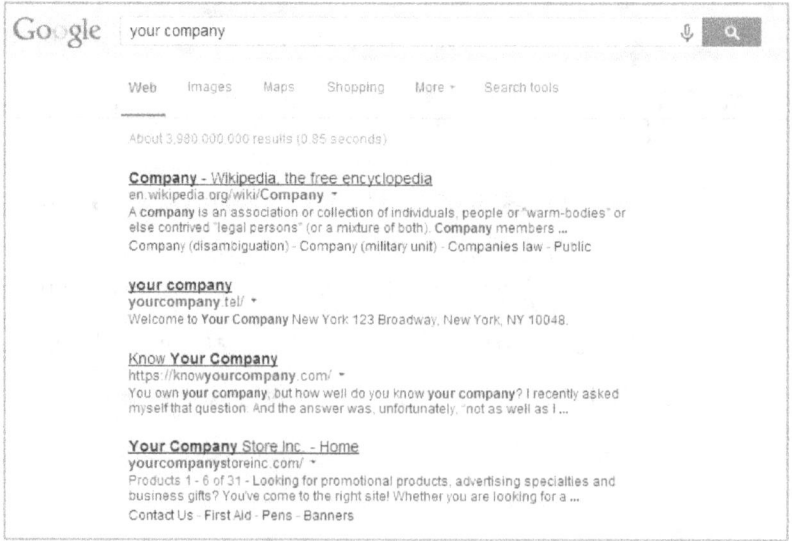

How to Create a Social Media Roadmap

Let's examine the big social media sites for each goal and see an overview of how they can help achieve your goals.

Build Credibility/Brand Exposure	Build Customer Relationships
LinkedIn Key word right profile – with picture! Create a mini company website Start a group – participate in a group Ask and answer questions **Twitter** Get involved in conversations Link to events, products, websites, press releases, articles Real time response **Facebook** Create a fan page Solicit feedback Contests to invite fans to share stories and/or photos Offer special fan coupons or online sales **YouTube** Show your products in action Brand your videos – create a TV channel	**LinkedIn** Ask/answer questions Establish yourself as an expert Research potential customers prior to making a call or visit **Twitter** Invite discussion Search for trending industry terms and get involved in conversations Real time response to unhappy customers Track conversations about competitors **Facebook** Giveaways Engage them in conversation Polls/surveys Contests Fill in the blank "I like your product because…." **YouTube** Entertain and inform Invite customer videos using your products Share mission/vision statements
Search Engine Optimization	**Drive Traffic to Your Website**
LinkedIn High ranking for organic search Link back to website/blog/Twitter accounts **Twitter** Full length URLs offer some SEO benefit **YouTube** Videos rank high, include full URL in video description **Flickr** Photos also rank high for links and key words Great for building inbound links which help with SEO	**LinkedIn** Not a high benefit however make sure your profile link to your website has been customized with the name of your company not just "website" **Twitter** Can drive traffic but keep the 80/20 rule in mind – talk more with others than about yourself. Use full URLs when possible **YouTube** Use full URL address in the description of each video

*Information found on CMO.com The Social Landscape

Using the information you have so far, select one focus for your social media participation. You may change it later, but this will give you a place to start when creating your Social Media Roadmap.

My primary goal

is..._____

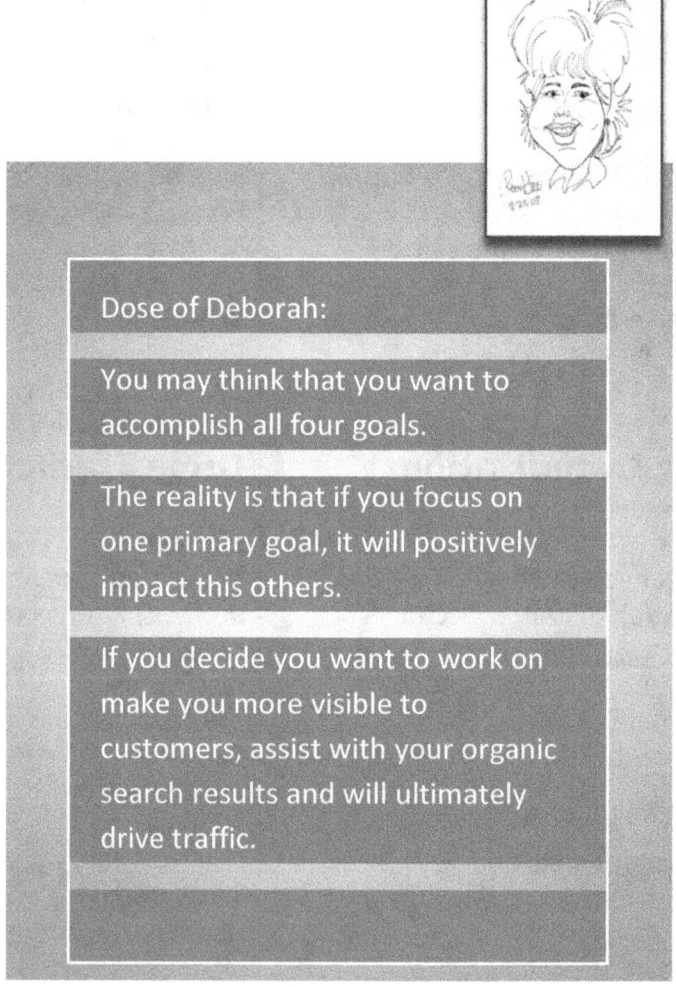

Dose of Deborah:

You may think that you want to accomplish all four goals.

The reality is that if you focus on one primary goal, it will positively impact this others.

If you decide you want to work on make you more visible to customers, assist with your organic search results and will ultimately drive traffic.

O: Originality
— what makes you unique in the industry? Why do your customers choose you? Are you an accountant? A business coach? A dentist? No matter what your profession or industry, you have competition. However, there are some things that set you apart. Spend some time on this worksheet by selecting a word that describes how you are unique. The alphabet forces you to be creative in your thinking. Once you use the "Q" for Quality and the "V" for Value-based – then what?

What makes my company unique is...

A		N	
B		O	
C		P	
D		Q	
E		R	
F		S	
G		T	
H		U	
I		V	
J		W	
K		X	
L		Y	
M		Z	

Deborah again: this may seem like a silly exercise and not one worth doing, but you'd be wrong. First off, complete this form with your team. It will make it easier and will also give you an idea of how your team views your business. You may be surprised by some of the words you come up with!

How to Create a Social Media Roadmap

A: Audience – describe your primary target audience.

Many businesses have more than one customer. Select the number one target audience that you are trying to do business with; describe them in detail. Gender, age, level of tech savvy, ability to say "yes," work title, industry, experience with your products.

When you are thinking of who your target audience is, actually pick one of your favorite customers. How did you connect with them? Do they use social media? Did they hear about you from a friend or find your website?

In some cases you may have different audiences. For example a home health care company would want to reach the children of aging adults who will use their services but they will also want to connect with social workers, doctors, nurses and other medical professionals.

I have provided two forms for you to complete. Think of your primary audience as the person(s) who will actually use your services/products. And the secondary audience as "centers of influence," the people who can refer your business to the end user.

My primary audience is…

Gender		Age Range	
Education		Career Type	
Income Range		Family Size	
What is their pain?		What key words will they search to find you?	

My secondary audience is…

Until you have a firm grasp of who you are trying to reach, you will not be able to connect with them on a truthful, authentic basis. Remember all of your competitors are out there trying to reach prospects too.

The better you understand who they are, where they hang out and what they need, the easier it will be to connect on a more personal level than just vendor and customer.

To make customers for life – you really have to focus on the relationship. More on that later.

Gender		Age Range	
Education		Career Type	
Income Range		Family Size	
What is their pain?		What key words will they search to find you?	

D: Direction –

What direction do you want the target audience to take – Call? Provide an email? Make a purchase? Click on your website? Attend your event?

> *"The success of a page should be measured by one criteria: Does the visitor do what you want them to do*
> *– Aaron Wall, SEObook.com*

Keep in mind, your target customer is the phone with only one interaction. Be prepared to be involved for the long haul. Only 2% of consumers will take action with only one visit.

What I want the reader to do next is…

Pick up the phone and call me	
Why?	
Send me an email	
For what purpose?	
Sign up for a class/webinar	
In person? Online?	
Is it developed yet?	
Is there a fee?	
Describe the program	
Make a purchase	
Do you have a store?	
Is it for a PDF?	
Is it special order	
Describe the item(s)	
Return frequently	
Why? What do you offer?	

Section Two: Examine the Roadmap Options

Let's examine the road options. Based on the goal that you have selected on previously, following is a chart that lists the most effective social media sites to assist you in achieving your goals.

For the purposes of being focused – circle the column heading that represents your initial focus.

Build Customer Relationships	Create Brand Awareness	Drive Traffic to Your Website	Improve Organic Search Results
Blogging	Press Releases	Blogging	Optimized Website
E-Newsletters	E-Newsletters	E-Newsletters	Google+
Facebook	Blogging	Twitter	Blogging
Twitter	LinkedIn	Facebook	Press Releases
YouTube	Twitter	Pinterest	E-Newsletters
Quora	Facebook	Reddit	Stumble Upon
Slideshare	Pinterest	Stumble Upon	YouTube
Google+	Slideshare		Flickr
	Instagram		
	Google+		
	Digg		

Looking down the list below your goal, are you currently on any of the sites listed?

Yes – I am on: (List your sites)

How often do you participate on those sites: (circle the answer that closely represents your activity)

Daily	Weekly	Monthly	Rarely

How often are you willing to participate on social media?

Daily	Weekly	Monthly	Rarely

Basics: Be an Option

Your website

Your company website is the first point of contact for your potential customer/client/patient/consumer.

So here is the first question and hopefully it won't be hard:

Do you have a website for your company?

Yes_____   No_____

> Dose of Deborah: Consumers use the Internet for all of their searches and research.
>
> If you aren't on the Internet – you don't exist.

If you do not have a website, what is holding you back?

- ☐ I don't see a need
- ☐ I just haven't gotten to it
- ☐ It is too overwhelming
- ☐ Other:_____

If you do have a website, when was the last time it was updated?

Check the answer that most represents your website:

- ☐ We update monthly
- ☐ It has been about a year
- ☐ It has been more than a year but we have updated since the original site
- ☐ It hasn't been updated since it first went live

Your website should be updated on a regular basis so that it remains high in the search rankings. Make sure that you have incorporated:

- Key word phrases
- Clear ways to contact you
- Call to action
- Geographic terms to help with local searches

Email marketing

Email marketing offers the best return on investment. A regular email campaign (at least monthly but no more frequently than weekly) has the benefit of:

- Keeping your name in front of prospects
- Providing value-based information
- Reinforcing your expertise
- Driving traffic to your website
- Sharing latest industry trend information
- Promoting a new product, service or event
- Giving readers a reason to call/contact you

If an email campaign is a project you are interested in pursuing, Mail Chimp is the suggested resource. It is a free email program for businesses with less than 2,000 email addresses. Mail Chimp also offers:

- Signup forms that can be added to your website to capture email addresses
- Ability to upload a large number of emails from an excel file
- Easy to use templates to create your newsletter
- Reports to show the effectiveness of your campaign individually and over time
- Automatic responding emails that can send information to new subscribers automatically

Online directories

One way to increase your visibility on the Internet is to ensure that your business is signed up for as many online directories as possible. Most directories, like Yellow Pages.com, Local.com and more allow you to "claim" your website and/or business address.

Look for the free option (several sites will try to sell you an upgraded listing but it isn't necessary) and then enter your business information.

Online directories will usually allow you the option of adding:

- Company name and address
- Phone number(s)
- Website address
- Hours of operation
- Business description
- Credit cards accepted

A few even allow you to connect additional information, photos or video to your directory listing.

Here are a few places you should start:

- Google Maps
- Yahoo
- Bing
- MSN
- Local
- Yellow Pages

David Gray has written an article with 101 Business Directories. (see next page)

The only cost is a time investment – but as long as your information remains the same, it is a "one and done" tasks.

David mentions using Yext.com to manage a large portion of your directories, however, there is a monthly fee.

I do recommend visiting Yext.com and inserting your company name – the report will give you a good place to start. However, be aware that they will begin emailing and calling you to encourage you to purchase their service. If you don't want to, just say no. They didn't insist.

How to Create a Social Media Roadmap

THE LIST: 101 ONLINE BUSINESS DIRECTORIES TO IMPROVE LOCAL SEARCH RANKINGS – DAVID GRAY

411.com *	HopStop.com *	PremierGuide
8coupons.com *	Hotfrog	ShowMeLocal.com *
About.me	Insider Pages	SuperMedia
Alike Nearby *	Instagram**	Superpages *
American Towns *	Judy's Book	Switchboard *
Angie's List	JustClickLocal.com	TeleAtlas
AOL Yellow Pages	Kudzu	ThinkLocal.com
AreaGuides.net	LinkedIn	Topix *
Avantar *	Local Database *	Totally Local
Better Business Bureau (BBB)	Local.com *	TripAdvisor
Best of the Web *	Localeze	Tupalo.com *
Bing	LocalNdex	Twibs
The Business Journals	LocalPages *	Twitter
BrownBook.net	Logal	US Yellow Pages
Bundle	MacRAE's Blue Book	USCity.net*
ChamberOfCommerce.com	MagicYellow	USDirectory.com
Citysearch *	Manta	Urbanspoon
CitySlick.net	MapQuest *	Verizon's 411
CitySquares*	Matchpoint	WhitePages*
CliqSearch *	MerchantCircle.com *	WhoWhere?
CoPilot Live*	Metrobot	Yahoo! *
Cricket's 411 *	MetroPCS 411 *	Yellow Assistance
DexKnows	MojoPages.com *	Yellowbook
DiscoverOurTown.com	Myspace*	YellowBot*
eLocal.com *	Navmii *	Yellowee
Yext.com	NAVTEQ Maps	Yellowise*
Express Update	Nokia Prime Place	YellowMoxie.com *
EZlocal.com *	DirectoryM	YellowPageCity.com *
Facebook	Oddpath	Yelp*
Factual *	Open List	YouTube
Foursquare*	Patch *	YP.com
Frontier Pages	Pinterest	Ypeek.com
GetFave.com *	PhoneNumber.com *	100. ZipLocal *
Google+	*(managed Yext.com)	101. ZipWeb

Before You Dismiss Hiring a Directory Service

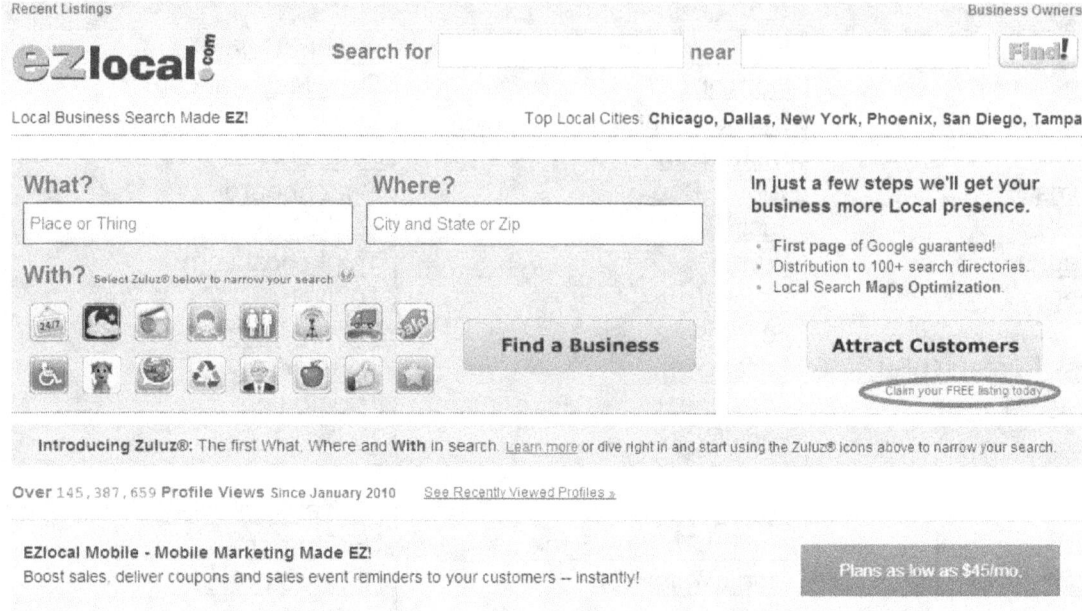

Finding how you register, claim or sign up your business for a free listing isn't always easy. Notice here on EZlocal.com how quietly they let you know where you click to claim your business.

However, if you look hard enough – you'll find it. Sometimes you have to look in the footer. Most times you will have to create an account before you can register your business; however, once you are successful, the listing is one more place that your business is listed with an inbound link to your website.

If you have access to a tech-savvy teen or college intern, this would be a great project to have them work on.

Make sure that you identify a few things in advance:

- Craft the description of your business so that it clearly identifies the products and services you offer.
- Create a listing of key words and phrases that you will want to include if given the option to add "tags." Tags are simply a listing of the key words people might search to find you.
- Agree on the industry you wish to be listed under. Some directories offer more choices than others but you will want to be consist with your listing.

- Be sure to include the http:// when adding your website URL to the directory listing. If you don't, the link to your website will not work.

The more work you complete in advance, the easier it will be to complete the different directory forms.

Press Releases

Keep in mind that writing a press release is no longer for the purpose of being printed in the local paper. Most local papers are shrinking and very few press releases that are submitted are ever printed.

However, a well written press release can have a very positive impact on your company's online visibility.

Keep in mind the following:

- The title is critical – similar to a subject line of an email, the title needs to be compelling enough for the person to want to read the article.
- Include geographical terms (city, county state) so that Google will improve your search results for people searching in your area.
- Remember to include the five Ws: who, what, where, when and why.
- Start the second paragraph with a quote from a reliable and authoritative source within your organization.
- Include contact information either at the top of the page or the bottom of the release so that people can quickly see who to call or email for more information.

> Dose of Deborah: Draw a line at the bottom of the second paragraph of your press release – if the reader only reads that far, will they catch the gist of the article?

Here are a few additional tips from Marketwire, a website dedicated to distributing news releases:

- Include your keyword phrase in the title
- Include the keyword phrase within the first 150 characters of your news article. Think the length of a Tweet – just about two sentences. This bullet point is 178 characters long.
- Include hyperlinked keyword phrases in your press release. A hyperlink is a word or group of words that when clicked on, take you to another web page.
- Use your targeted key word phrase in the first hyperlink.
- The pages that you link to, load quickly and the links are correct.
- Your key words phrases shouldn't be over used within the body of your text or in the number of your hyperlinks. Marketwire recommends that your "target keyword phrase be less than or equal to 5% of all words used in your release."

Create an Editorial Calendar

Creating an Editorial Calendar for your content is the best way to ensure you have a plan for what you'll publish. The Internet is a demanding mistress; it requires regular feeding and your best search engine results will be found through the effective use of consistent value-based informational articles.

In comparison to social media where potential customers have to find you, a press release or a newsletter will find them by appearing in their local paper, online news magazines or email box.

Note: Some businesses that feel they aren't quite ready for a full blown Social Media Roadmap because they believe their target customers aren't using the "big three," may opt to just create a strategic plan using these more traditional forms of marketing communication.

To learn more about creating an editorial calendar, pick up my workbook:

How to Create an Editorial Calendar for Press Releases, Newsletters and Articles

Now available from Amazon.

The "Social Media" Part of the Social Media Roadmap

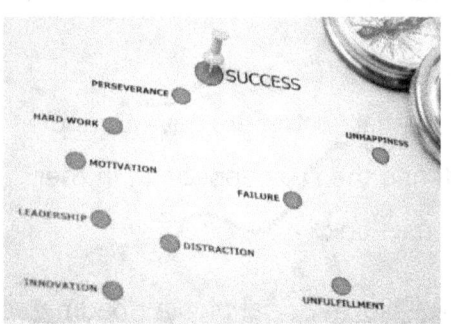

It is now time to explore the actual social media sites that you may choose to add to your Social Media Roadmap.

There are two directions for content on the Internet:

   Push content out to consumers.

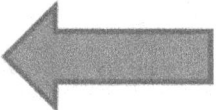

Rely on consumers finding you.

So far we have focused on the ways to push content into the email boxes of your target prospect. Press releases, enewsletters, etc. are all great ways to share valuable information with your prospects. In fact, as I mentioned before, enewsletter have the highest rate of return because they are dangled in the face of consumers as opposed to being found on LinkedIn, Twitter and Facebook.

However, the social sites where consumers can find you are also of critical importance because of the sheer volume of hours people spend every day "googling," "facebooking" and "pinning."

Casual Communicator

Let's start with the casual communicator. If your target audience is young, by that I mean under 30, they spend a lot of time on sites designed for a more social and casual encounter.

Although you may find Baby Boomers on Facebook – and it is the fastest rising population on the billion-participant social site, they usually are there to share images, opinions and jokes. They may not looking for a vendor or networking with other business professionals.

If you are retailer or a restaurant, Facebook is the right place to spend your time.

However if you are a B2B or seek the C Suite of an organization for business networking (C Suite = CEO, COO, CIO, CMO, etc.) then trying to build a business on Facebook my not be the best use of your time and energy.

There are as many "how to" articles on using Facebook for business as there are Facebook users so I won't take the time to try and improve on what has already been written. However, if you are wondering if Facebook is right for you, take this little quiz:

Is Facebook Right for Your Business?

- Is my ideal prospect actively involved in using Facebook?
- Do I have a staff member available and willing to post daily (or more frequent) posts that engage the audience?
- Do I have an ever changing product to promote such as menu items, new inventory, daily specials, coupons, etc.
- Am I willing to post pictures of consumers, products and events that can be shared and commented on?
- Does my target audience have the ability to say yes to a purchase and the available funds to make a purchase? (example, you may attract teens to your page but do they have disposable income or transportation?)
- Am I willing to spend marketing dollars to promote my business on Facebook

If you answered yes to two or more questions then perhaps Facebook is a social site you might consider has part of your overall social media roadmap.

Survey Says...

Here is a survey done by Multi Briefs that strongly suggests Facebook ads are not the be all and end l of reaching your ideal prospects.

EXCLUSIVE CONTENT

March 16, 2014

Quick Links >

Social media advertising Results

1. Does your business advertise on Facebook?
   11 responses:
   Yes, and it's very effective
   1 (9%)
   Yes, but we've seen little ROI
   5 (45%)
   No, but we're considering it
   5 (45%)
   No, it's not the right audience
   (0%)

FINAL FACEBOOK NOTE:

The days of FREE are over. Be prepared to dedicate cold hard cash if you want your company page to appear in the news feed of your followers. The changes in Facebook in 2014 now require you to spend cash to find any real benefit on this social network.

How to Create a Social Media Roadmap

Facebook To-Do

✓ Item

- [ ] Sign into Facebook
- [ ] Select to use Facebook as Your Company Page
- [ ] Check for new likes, comments, notifications and emails
- [ ] Respond to them.
- [ ] Share a status update about your company – link to your website/blog/video
- [ ] Ask a question (If someone handed you $10,000 today to use on your business – how would you spend it?)
- [ ] Click on the Home button in upper right corner
- [ ] Scroll the news feed for interesting articles from pages you follow as a company
- [ ] If you don't follow any pages – while signed in as your company – visit industry Facebook pages and click Like
- [ ] Look for articles of interest to your community. Share on your page
- [ ] Add your comment
- [ ] Visit the pages of industry leaders and centers of influence.
- [ ] As your company page – leave a comment – join a discussion – ask a question
- [ ] Change your Facebook use to your personal page and share updates from the company page onto your personal page.
- [ ] **Thursday:** This is #TBT Throwback Thursday. A great way to share images of your business, products from a long time ago.

www.TheSocialMediaRoadmap.com
Copyright 2014

 Have you heard of Tumblr? If you are under 25 or a celebrity, you probably spend most of your time on this social site.

Why Tumblr?

Well, for one thing, parents haven't figured it out and they are still stalking their children on Facebook.

Secondly, it is a hip, quick way to communicate and combines several social functions in one. Tumblr is a blog, video, photo and Twitter platform rolled into one. Here is my page: Social Media Roadmap.

You can see from the prompt at the top of the page that I can select to share:

- Text
- Photos
- Quotation
- Link
- Chat
- Audio
- Video

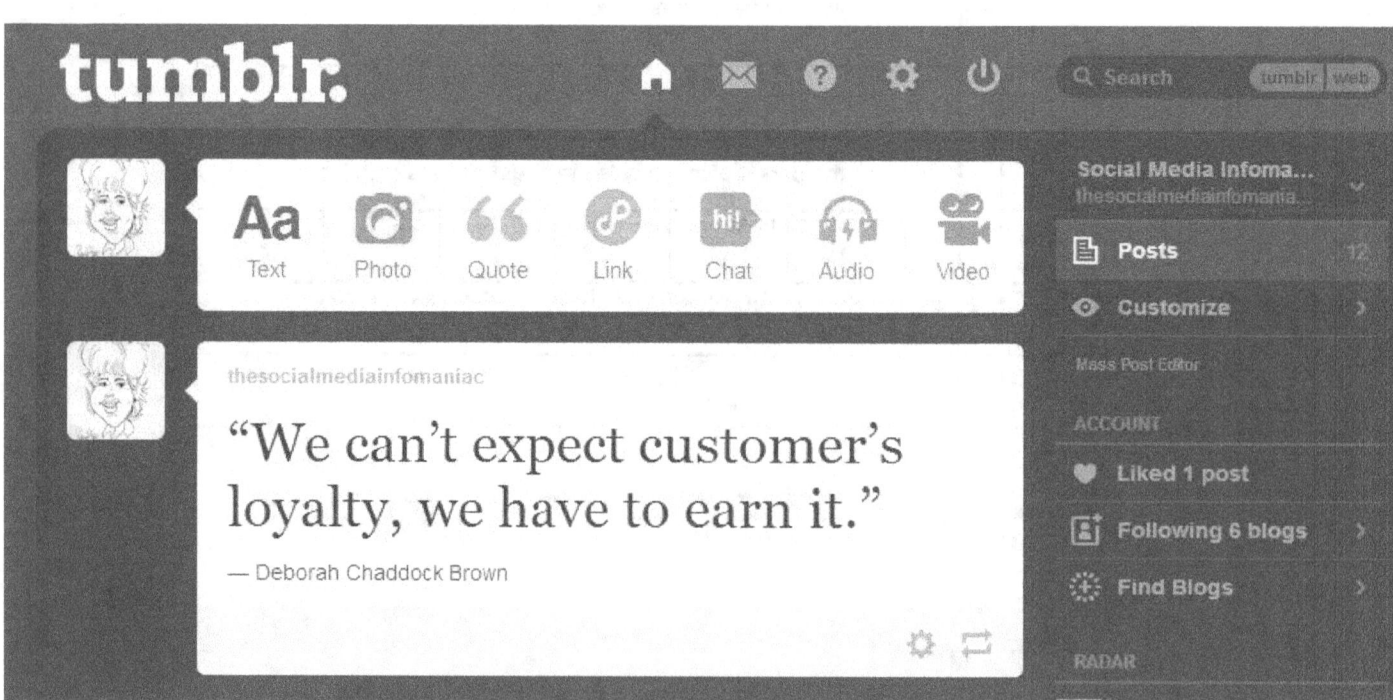

Do I recommend Tumblr?

If you have teens, I recommend you follow your child and be aware of what they are talking about and who they are connecting to.

Do I think it is a great place for your business? Unless you are catering to the teens, my answer is no. Here is an example. In a search for pizza restaurants, rather than seeing company names you might recognize like Pizza Hut, Dominos and Papa Johns', I find Tumblr accounts dedicated to a love of pizza and individual posts of people chowing down.

Let's tumble past Tumblr and check out our professional options, shall we?

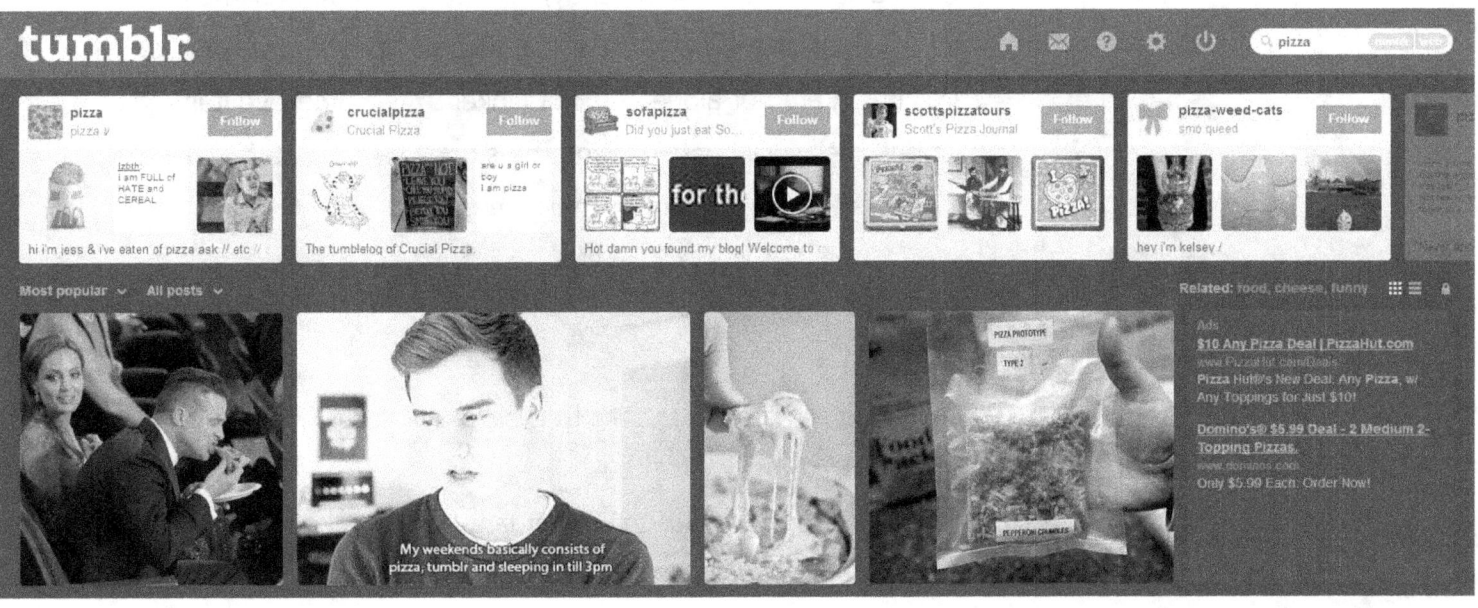

Professional Networker

Ahhh, my comfort zone. This is where I live and where most business professionals should be as well.

Do you sell insurance, offer real estate services? Coach professionals? Offer marketing services? Design marketing materials? Support the healthcare industry? Work with property managers? Seek a connection with business owners, financial leaders, operational managers and human resource directors?

The following social networks should be on your roadmap.

I spent a little bit of time recently, searching the web for the latest stats on LinkedIn; my favorite social media network for business. Turns out, I am not alone, 73% of LinkedIn users believe it is the best business social network and the survey says….B2B businesses may get the biggest bang for their time.

- 53% of B2B users have actually gained a customer thanks to their ongoing relationship building efforts on LinkedIn. That is a significant number.
- 4 out of 5 LinkedIn users are the decision makers for their company, lets you know that your time on the network could lead to additional business.
- 83% of B2B marketers use LinkedIn for business

So just how effective are you on LinkedIn?

- Do you get involved in discussions within groups?
- Do you actively grow your network, seeking out relationships with centers of influence?
- Do you use the search function to find the right person to connect with or to learn more about someone prior to your first in person meeting?

How to Create a Social Media Roadmap

- Do you use the poll function to ask open ended questions of your network so that you gain a better understanding of their needs and concerns?
- Do you engage in conversation via the daily status updates, share articles and videos of value?
- Have you created a company page for your business and share company updates with those that follow your page?

LinkedIn is a powerful network for your business and can take the place of other, less effective messages of research.

9 Annoying LinkedIn Habits That Turn off Prospects

LinkedIn is the number one business networking site on the Internet today. It isn't just a tool for those looking for work but can be used to enhance your personal brand, seek new clients or grow your community.

However just as quickly as you reinforce your expert status in your industry, a few wrong moves can permanently damage how you are viewed in the business world.

We have become a society of short attention span, information seekers and make judgments in the blink of an eye. Following are nine things that business professionals do on LinkedIn that turn that "blink" into a "wince," forever tarnishing your brand on social media.

1. **No picture or unprofessional photo:** in business, building trust is a critical component of success and so if your picture is either missing, is a company logo or a cartoon Avatar, it tells those visiting your LinkedIn profile a few things:

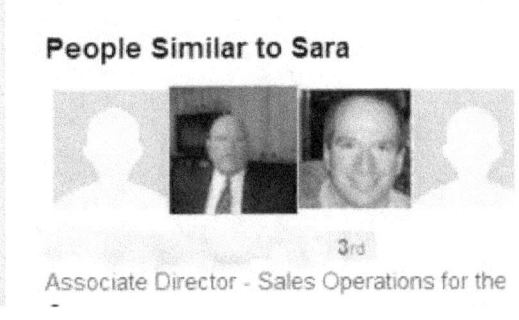

- You are hiding something
- You have little or no self confidence
- You are lazy
- You don't care enough about your brand to include a photo
- You are so ugly, you have broken the camera

2. Generic **title that tells me nothing about what you do:** the words under your name are the most important words in your LinkedIn profile. What does yours say? If you have used the words Manager, Owner, President, Director, or some other title that really belongs in the Professional Experience section of your profile. Think of these 125 characters as a billboard for why someone should connect with you.

3. **Stringing words together that aren't searchable:** this is also called keyword stuffing and looks something like this: WHAT?

4. **All caps in your name and/or headline:** please don't shout at me. Current social media, email and text etiquette states that when you use all CAPS in your communication it is perceived as yelling; often with an angry tone. Take the time to correctly type the information into your profile using big and little letters where appropriate.

5. **Generic invitations:** this is a huge no-no. Yes, LinkedIn makes it easy to invite another business professional to connect by automatically filling in the content of your message, but how lazy is that? The only thing worse is sending an invite when your profile doesn't have a picture.

It now requires that the receiver of your invitation know you really well. Take the time to write one or two sentences that explain your desire to connect.

Even if you just went golfing with them last week – show them the courtesy of personalizing your message. See how the personalized message stands out from all of the generic ones in the picture above? Here are some examples of what you could say:

- "Your name just appeared on my LinkedIn home page and I was surprised to find out that we aren't connected."
- "I'm looking forward to our business call later this week and thought we should be connected on LinkedIn."
- "I enjoyed your workshop at the Chamber and would very much appreciate being part of your LinkedIn network."
- "We haven't met but your name came up in a Chamber meeting and I'd love to connect and learn more about what you do."
- "I was searching for people in your industry and you came up at the top of the search results.

6. **Saying I'm your friend in your invitation:** when you send an invitation, you are given a few options and if you haven't worked with the person the knee jerk reaction is to select "friend." There is nothing that ticks me off faster than someone saying they are my friend when we've never met. Add a generic message and a profile with no picture and I'm seeing red! Select "Colleague" and click on your current title and then be specific in the invitation as to how you know them or why you want to.

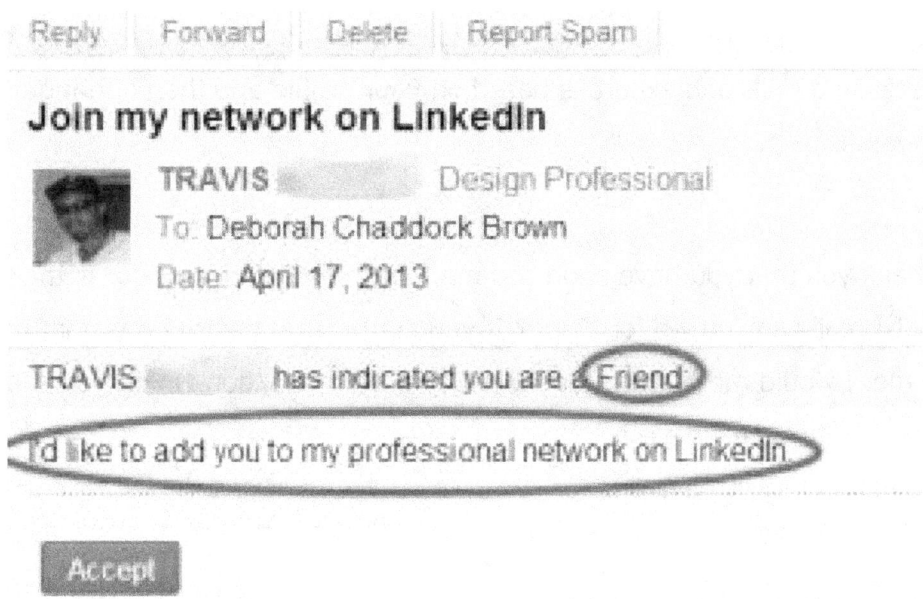

7. **Incomplete profile:** again, just how serious are you about participating in the largest business networking site in the world? Set aside some time and fill out your profile! LinkedIn makes it easy to, not only add your job history, but include your charitable efforts, published articles, photos, videos and slide presentations and more to your profile.

8. **Sales pitch status updates/group conversations:** yes I know you have to make a living, but don't be constantly shoving your sales pitch down my throat. I want to learn more about what you value and find interesting so share articles and videos that you've encountered and then tell me what you liked about them. Shine the spotlight on others and take the time to comment on what I'm doing as well. Create a name for yourself as someone who cares about more than just your own bottom line.

9. **Endorsing me for something I don't do:** Linked has created a lazy way to recommend someone by selecting skills and expertise based on your profile and then offering options that others can endorse.

Okay, I say thank you that you have endorsed me, but think before you do. Is the skill something that I really am known for doing? If you are unsure, please don't confuse my brand by endorsing me. I would rather you actually left a recommendation where you shared your thoughts on my abilities. Leave me a recommendation...and I will leave one for you!

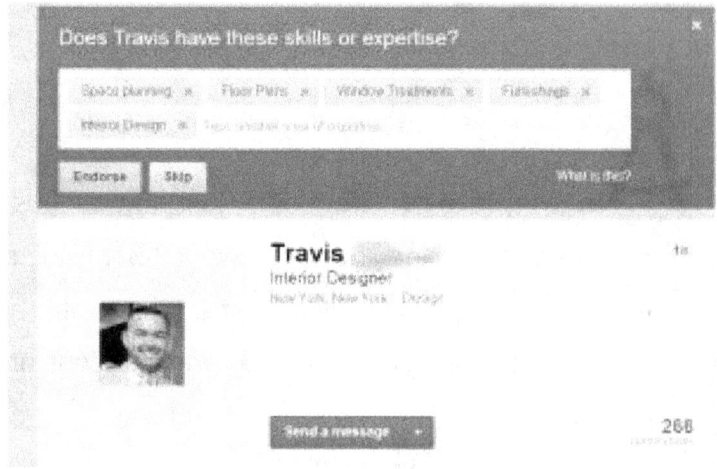

You can see how easily we can offend or turn off potential business leaders with a few short cuts. Remember, this is your brand. You are essentially your own best product so make sure that you take the time to represent yourself professionally.

How Do I Handle LinkedIn Invitations?

I recently was asked this question: **When I receive an invitation on LinkedIn and I don't know the person — what should I do?**

The first question I ask back is "What are you using LinkedIn to do for your business?" If the answer is that you want to build a strategic network to help uncover leads to grow your business and to build your own personal brand awareness, than I share my personal process.

When I receive an invitation on LinkedIn for a person that I don't know, I first review their profile:

- **Where are they located?** Are they in my geographical area and so perhaps we have met or they are someone I should know. If they are out of state, what possible interest do they have in connecting with me and is there a benefit to connecting with them?
- **Do we share connections?** Are we connected through people I really know or people I admire in the industry that we've both connected to because we read their blog or book?
- **Did they send a generic invite?** Hate those. If someone can't take the time to customize their email then I am afraid it is a little black mark against them. If they KNOW they don't know me but want to connect, then please take the time to explain WHY you want to connect.
- **Do they have a picture?** A profile that doesn't have a picture says that they aren't serious about connecting, they are dabbling in LinkedIn and don't understand it's benefits and they may even be hiding something. I know that sounds like a stretch, but you build relationships based on trust and not sharing your picture is a lack of trust.
- **What industry are they in?** Do we do the same thing? Are they in an industry that I'm trying to tap into? Are they attending college. (as an aside, if they are attending college — I connect and offer to help in my follow up email)

If we share connections, they explained themselves more thoroughly in the invite and I have an interest in their business field, I accept and then send a personal note thanking them and asking a few more questions.

If we share connections and they sent a generic message, I reply without accepting and ask how we know each other. I say something like "Thanks so much for reaching out. Help me remember how we know each other." Often they were in the audience for one of my speeches. If they respond – they really want to connect and so I accept. If they don't respond – and they are out of the NE Ohio region – I figure they just wanted to mine my contacts. If they are local and don't respond, I figure they don't know how to use LI and I don't accept.

Follow Up Is Key to Building Business Connections

Every time I accept an invitation, I follow up with a personal message. I thank them for their connection and ask how I can help. If there is something major missing on their profile (like a picture) or an opportunity for them to improve their profile (customizing their LinkedIn URL for example) I also share those tips.

The value in your LinkedIn contacts is the relationship that you build so take the time to reach out with personal messages not just the generic, auto fill text provided by LinkedIn. When you connect "real person" to "real person" you'll find much more value in your LinkedIn experience.

Final Thoughts on LinkedIn

- Be on it.
- Join groups.
- Create a company page.
- Leave Status Updates.
- Comment on other people's articles
- Keep your profile updated
- Continually build your network
- Research the companies you admire.

If you still are not sure how to use LinkedIn to its fullest – seek out someone who can help.

Pick me! Pick me! Deborah@allwriteink.com

LinkedIn To-Do List

✓	Item
☐	Sign into LinkedIn
☐	Check your In Box for new Invitations or Emails and respond
☐	Review your news feed for interesting articles, changes in your network, new posts or discussions
☐	Add a comment, like or share
☐	Repeat as necessary
☐	Share a status update and link to an article, web page, event page, video that you found of value
☐	Make sure you comment about why you found it of interest
☐	Review the 3 names of People You May Know
☐	Select one and review their profile
☐	Send a personalized invitation to connect to at least one
☐	Visit at least one group
☐	Review the most recent discussions, select one and add to the conversation
☐	Visit one company page (your own if applicable)
☐	Share a status update (if it is your own page)
☐	Comment, like or share an article that is posted on a company page you follow

www.TheSocialMediaRoadmap.com
Copyright 2014

 Google+ is the new kid on the block. It is Google's answer to Facebook and LinkedIn combined. So if it is a duplicate, why should you care?

Because it is Google.

Google+ is the latest in social networks available for small business owners to connect with their community. Google+ is similar to Facebook in that it has a chronological newsfeed offering the latest articles video and comments from people within your community.

Google+ is also like LinkedIn in that it is a business community of owners, professionals, and entrepreneurs who are seeking connection with other business professionals.

The intriguing main benefit of Google+ is the fact that it is in fact a Google product. Google is the number one search engine claiming almost 80% of all searches around the world. Therefore, participating in a social network that is managed by the number one search engine is definitely a benefit for your personal brand and your business.

Building Your Google+ Community

Building a community with Google+ is slightly different from other venues in that you do not need to ask permission to join someone's network.

Google+ Personal Profile: Google+ allows you the opportunity to create a personal profile page in which you build a profile that includes a professional, as well as information about your professional life and personal interests.

Google+ Company Page: For business owners, you are also able to create a Google+ page that focuses on your business. The separation of profile page and personal page is similar to the LinkedIn profile and Company page experience. When leaving comments from your company page the author is the company, when leaving comments from your personal profile page, you are the author.

Google Authorship: Google+ has initiated an author ship program which focuses on having participants connect their authentic, value-based, new information to their Google+ profile so that it can be shared with their community. Visit https://plus.google.com/authorship to connect your blogs and websites to your Google+ profile.

Dose of Deborah: I have got to be honest...I still struggle with the benefits of this site with the exception of the fact that your updates are indexed as part of the Google Search.

However, check out Google Hangouts – this is a real benefit and you can easily video tape the sessions and then post them on YouTube.

Company Blog is #1 for Your Social Media Roadmap

STOP: Don't close this workbook. I know you don't want to hear that you need a blog for your business; it is too big of a commitment, you don't like to write and even if you did, what would you write about?

Okay – I totally understand your hesitation and I completely understand the concept of "not enough hours in the day," but before you totally dismiss this all important component of your Roadmap, listen to Denise Wakeman of The Blog Squad share her thoughts on the subject:

5 Essential Elements for Your Visibility Plan – Denise Wakeman

1. **Blog** – this is a no-brainer. You absolutely must have a piece of digital real estate you own and control. This is where all traffic is directed as you build your audience. This is where you post the search-engine friendly content that helps you get found by those searching for the solution you and your book offer.

Read about all five tips from Denise here: Build a Foundation to Sell More Books.

Why a Blog?

A blog is the perfect opportunity to share your knowledge and expertise and to engage your audience in conversation. Most blogs share an opinion or raise a question which invites the reader to agree or disagree. Your website is written as a corporate marketing piece – polished and formal. Information shared without an opportunity to interact.

A blog is written in a more personal voice, it is topical, current, sometimes controversial but always a open door for customers and prospects to comment.

The most successful blogs are timely and informative – not just sales messages that drive traffic back to your website. Website writers understand the value of well written web content, but also the importance of that personal connection in a blog. Two different types of writing style.

How to Create a Social Media Roadmap

Denise Wakeman was a guest on our weekly online radio show and she shared some information about the benefit a blog brings to a business. Following are notes from the interviews, but I invite you to listen to the complete 30 minute show.

http://www.blogtalkradio.com/usmedia/2011/05/24/us-media-radio--denise-wakeman-on-blogging

Quick Stats on Company Blogs from Denise Wakeman

- 48% of people on the web will get their news and information from blogs.
- Blogs have really matured into a media channel with readers getting and trusting information as much as from their friends.
- More than 50% read a blog at least monthly.
- Companies who use blogs attract 55% more visitors to their website than companies who don't use a blog. If your business can not be found on the web, you don't exist.
- Use your blog like a hub on your web, you can go deep and intimate as well as be findable.
- It's your virtual real estate that you own and control.

Why do you need a blog if you have a Facebook?

Facebook is not the house. You don't control Facebook, Facebook belongs to Facebook. You use Facebook to attract those people back to your home base, your blog.

On the web you want to actively demonstrate your expertise and display your personality, your audience gets to know you trust you and like you and then decide if they want to work with you.

Blogging takes time and commitment

Blog is a marketing tool. Do you have time to market your business? Blogging is the best because it works for you 24/7. Content that you're creating shows your credibility, is search engine indexed and demonstrates your expertise. When you write about your industry in a captivating compelling way, each new blog post is a new path to your door.

It's not about writing on your blog, it's about marketing your business.

Things to consider before starting your company blog:

- Purpose of blog – thought leadership, write a book,
- Goals for the blog – build list , sell products/ sell services
- What do you want the reader to do. If no call to action, you're wasting your time.
- What's your primary topic: one subject and subtopics.
- Create an editorial calendar and plan out your articles
- 4 e's : Educate, entertain, engage and enrich. That will guide your content.
- Be Consistent. Every 3 weeks is not enough, not compelling enough to get readers to come back and discover more about your expertise.

Steps for Starting a Blog:

Who is your audience? –are you writing for people who do what you do, or for the people who want to hire you.

Focus on the potential clients. Your niche will generally be your ideal client.

Build your content and then lead them to your call to action:

- Appropriate download report
- Buy your new product
- Buy your new service
- Enroll in your new webinar
- Sign up for your newsletter.

Your blog post title is basically the headline. The first and maybe the ONLY impression on your reader. So your headline is very important.

When you syndicate your content (like twitter, RSS, Facebook and LinkedIn) your reader will only see the title as the link. So that will determine if they retweet or share your link.

___ out of 10 read the headline. Only 2 out of 10 will read the rest.

STATS show posts with numbers will bring in more traffic. People like easy to digest content. Like something very specific and they know it is digestible, bite size chunks and easy for them to consume.

Consistency. Started with every weekday, then 3 times. If you've neglected, should you backfill, or just admit you took a break.

Dose of Deborah: I have to be honest – I struggle with my blog. I have created and abandoned six blogs since 2005. However, I keep going back and starting over.

Currently I have a blog associated with AllWriteink.com and one with TheSocialMediaRoadmap.com. Rather than kick myself for not writing every day or every week, I make sure that I write when I have something worth sharing.

Then I use that content to post on all of my social media sites.

Typically 2-3 times a week minimum. Your audience will tell you if it is too little, they won't come back, too much, they unsubscribe.

What do you do when you abandon your blog

Back date doesn't' help. Just start posting all over again. If topic has changed, maybe start a fresh blog if your demographic has changed. Audience specific. Don't apologize, or back pedal. Just start posting again. Quick relevant useful information that makes your life easier. The more you post, the more traffic you're going to get.

Visual Spirit

Pinterest

Pinterest is essentially an online scrapbook that you can share.

It started as a place that crafters, photographers, interior designers and artists gravitated to because it is IMAGE HEAVY. By that, I mean that everything you post is a picture.

Along with an image you can also add a brief description, organize your images by category and even include a link back to your website. Within seconds this social site eclipsed Facebook in usage and people were hooked. By people, I basically mean women. This site is heavily dominated by women.

As Pinterest grew in popularity, the owners saw an opportunity to capture the business audience and added reporting and the ability to link or PIN your website images to your Pinterest account and vice versa.

Additionally, if you are selling a product, include a price point within the description and connect the image to a purchase page.

In 2014 Pinterest boasted the highest rate of click through to purchase of any social site!

How to Create a Social Media Roadmap

You Don't Have to Sell Product to Use Pinterest

As the site grew in popularity, businesses who offer services rather than products have also found a way to create a brand on this image-based website. In 2014 CMO.com (Chief Marketing Organization) listed Pinterest on their Social Landscape Guide as a valuable site to:

- Improve search engine optimization
- Create brand awareness for your business
- Generate additional traffic to your website

Following are steps to setting up your Pinterest account.

- **Settings**
- You can work on your account before shouting to the world (and Google) that your page is live.
- Click on Settings and complete the form:
    - Look for "Search Privacy" and keep the box on NO until you are ready to tell the world
    - Determine when you would like to receive notifications. The yes/no box is available for each time someone interacts with you on Pinterest. This setting can be readjusted if you find you are receiving too many emails.
- **Board strategy**: Create individual boards for each service/product/interest. I.e. a jewelry company might create the following boards:
    - Bracelets
    - Necklaces
    - Rings
    - Gifts for women
    - Artistic design
    - Gemstones
    - History of jewelry
    - Precious metals
    - Jewelry for girls

How to Create a Social Media Roadmap

- **Boards "how to":** When you create the board remember the following:
    - Name the board with a specific key word(s)
    - Include a description of the board that tells the viewer more than just "this is a board about bracelets." Include your keywords. If your bracelets are primarily sterling silver, include that phrase. If they are handcrafted, American made, etc.
    - Pin pictures from your own collection and repin images from others on Pinterest that are focused on the theme of that board.
- **Pin images** from your own computer:
    - Click Add a Pin
    - Locate a photo from your computer files
    - Select the correct board from the drop down box
    - Add a description – include the following:
        - Three or four sentences telling about the image
        - Key words
        - #specific key words to improve search
        - http://yoururl.com that corresponds with the image
        - $9.99 a price if the item is available for sale
        - Hit PIN IT
        - The picture will appear on the board – click the EDIT button
        - In the next box – include a URL for the image:
            - If it is a book available from Amazon, include the page in Amazon the book can be found
            - If it is for sale from your website, include the link that will take them directly to the purchase page
        - Share the image – click the appropriate social media buttons to share your image on other sites.
- **Search Pinterest for other pins**
    - Type a phrase in the search bar that corresponds to one of your boards
        - Find Pins, Boards and/or People
        - Look for Pins (images) that complement your board without being a direct competition. Jewelry example – look for hair ornaments, scarves, purses, other accessory items.

- Click PIN
- Select the appropriate board
- Add to the description or not
- Go back to the original image and leave a comment. (most people miss this step and it puts your name in front of the Pinner and will hopefully increase traffic to your page.)
    - Pin from the Web.
        - When you find an image, infographic, article or video that you like – consider pinning it to one of your boards. Most will have Pin option.
        - If an article does not have the Pin option:
            - copy the URL
            - Go into your Pinterest account and select Add a Pin
            - Select From URL
            - Paste the URL into the box and continue as normal

- **Find Friends**
    - Increase traffic to your boards by first following others.
    - If you set up your account through Twitter/Facebook – Pinterest will connect with your accounts and seek out people you current follow in social media that are also on Pinterest. (Go to Settings – Find Friends)
    - If you set up your account with an email – manually search for people using the search bar.

- **Website Connection**
    - Include a Pinterest icon on your website and blog to ensure people visiting your sites click and follow your page.
    - Consider editing your website images to point to a corresponding Pin on Pinterest (do this by changing the linking URL of the image to Pinterest)

Pinterest Tips

- Check to see if your company website has already been pinned by others:
  - www.pinterest.com/source/yourdomainname.com
- Convert your Pinterest page to the new business page:
  - www.business.pinterest.com
- Key words are the most important – use the same key word phrases you are using on your website and blog. Not sure which words to use? Check out the Google Keyword Tool.
  - https://adwords.google.com/o/Targeting/Explorer?_c=1000000000&_u=1000000000&ideaRequestType=KEYWORD_IDEAS (or search for Google Keyword tool)
- Link Pinterest to Facebook COMPANY page:
  - www.woobox.com/pinterest
- Tall or long images are more popular and capture the attention more than a regular sized image.

Five Pin Ideas from Entrepreneur Academy:

1. **Infographics.** This are incredibly popular and frequently repined. Create your own for free:
   a. www.infogr.am
2. **Checklists.** People love a list of things to do, a list of great books, a list of top Twitter accounts to follow – create a list that corresponds with your business. Save the list as an image and pin to your page.
3. **Tutorials.** Instruction pins have a higher CTR (click through rate) than most pins. Think of a DIY tutorial that you can provide for your readers.
4. **Pins with Text (MEME).** This is simply a picture with words. You'll find these frequently on Facebook. To create a Meme visit:
   a. www.picmonkey.com
5. **Videos.** If you have videos on YouTube, these make great pins that are frequently repined:
   a. Find the video on Youtube.
   b. Click on the share button
   c. Find the social media icons – if Pinterest isn't visible – click on the arrow or "more" options to find the P.
   d. Click on the P for Pinterest and select the appropriate board (you may want to create a special Video board)

YouTube

Statistics on the web change hourly, but in early 2014 the website Digital Marketing Ramblings:

http://expandedramblings.com/index.php/youtube-statistics/

Created a listing of 36 YouTube stats. Here are just a few that will blow your mind:

YouTube Stats from DMR

- Number of YouTube users: 1 BILLION
- Total YouTube views in 2011: 1 TRILLION
- Number of YouTube video views per day: 4 billion
- Hours of video watched per month on YouTube: 6 billion
- Videos uploaded to YouTube per minute: 100 hours
- Average YouTube mobile video views per day: 1 billion
- Percentage of YouTube traffic from mobile: 40%
- Percentage of Americans that use YouTube during working hours: 14.4%

The numbers are staggering. Add to that the fact that top marketers have predicted that video is overtaking written content – consumers want to be shown, not told.

What Does That Mean for Your Business?

You need to start uploading videos.

A great tool for creating 30 second videos is Animoto.com. In a matter of minutes you can take a few images and some text and Animoto will create an animated video with music (or your original uploaded audio) that you can easily share on YouTube, Facebook or your website.

You can also take a video of your business, a speaking engagement, a customer's testimonial and create a short 6 second gif – a piece of video that automatically repeats. These are very popular and often become viral.

Visit imgflip.com and up load a video. It will then allow you to select a section of the video to turn into a gif.

YouTube now also offers a gif creator application. Once you have uploaded the video to YouTube, using their tool, select a section of the video to turn into a repeating piece of animation.

Upload these to:

- Vine
- Funny Vids
- Facebook
- Twitter
- LinkedIn
- Embed into your blog or website
- Share with your audience via an email blast

Make sure you incorporate key words into your video description, use #hashtag key words and include a link to your website. Make it easy for people to follow up and learn more.

Dose of Deborah: You don't have to spend thousands of dollars on a professional video. Use your camera or the webcam on your computer to create short, informative videos that you can share.

One of the most searched phrases on YouTube is "how to" — what kind of "how to" video can you create for your business?

Memes

A meme is an image with words over top; usually a quote, inspirational saying or words of wisdom. Here are a few examples:

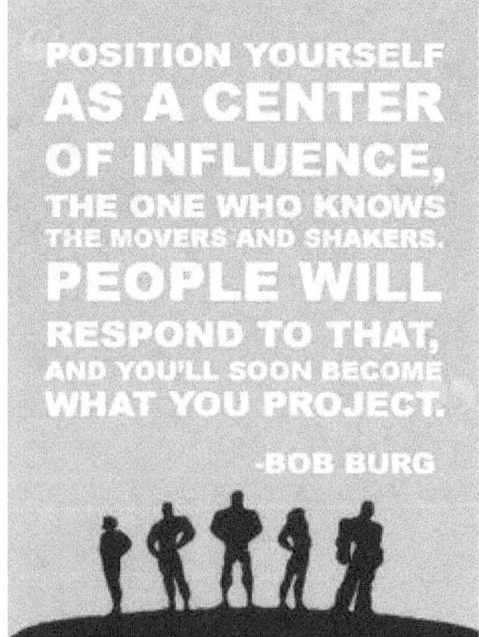

To create a meme you can:

• Visit picmonkey.com and upload an image and add text over top.

• Visit imgflip.com and upload a photo. This site allows you to put words and the top and bottom of the page. Make sure you save on your computer before using.

QR Tags/Codes

I sure you have seen this blocks of dots, perhaps in a magazine, on a postcard or even on a residential for sale sign, but you may not understand the purpose.

Each unique block of dots, when a user takes a picture of it with their smart phone, takes them to a webpage. You can program the QR Tags to take a visitor to a video, a newsletter signup page or the home page of your website.

QR tags are simple to create, just visit a free QR tag creation site such as:

QR Stuff: http://www.qrstuff.com/

QR Code: http://qrcode.kaywa.com/

QR Code Generator: http://www.qr-code-generator.com/

They are all free and allow you to create a QR tag for

Websites	Newsletter sign up forms
Videos	Email address
LinkedIn	Phone numbers
Twitter	Map
Facebook	Events and more

Use the QR Tab on your business cards, flyers, social media sites, trade show displays. It is a quick and mobile way to quickly connect your customers with a specific portion of your business.

Instantaneous Sharer

Twitter

Some time around 2008 I attended a web marketing luncheon to hear what the trends were. Most of social media was still very new and I went because the agenda was to include the benefits of Twitter. At the time, I thought it was just some stupid name.

The speaker, Pete Radke, talked about the Minneapolis bridge collapse. It was a tragic event but what he wanted to share was how Twitter really changed the way we handle major life events.

He said that it took news crews 22 minutes to get to the bridge but within minutes of the bridge collapsing, people actually on the bridge had been able to tweet their status and location. Within minutes.

You might say, well, they could have texted. Yes, but who would that reach? One person, perhaps a handful, but with Twitter, the message was sent out to thousands.

Okay, Twitter is Amazing, What Does That Mean For Me?

It has been several years since the bridge incident and hundreds of millions of people now embrace this real time social tool; most notably celebrities and politicians. Great, but again, what should you care, am I right?

Twitter is real time and because of that immediacy you can use the tool to listen. You don't have to always be the talker, the promoter, the marketer, the sales person. Sometimes we learn the most when we shut our mouths and open our ears. At least that is what my first grade teacher told me.

How to Create a Social Media Roadmap

When we listen we learn:

- What interests our customers
- What our competitors are talking about
- Who is unhappy with our products and services

- Who had a great experience
- About new product offerings our customers want/need
- The latest industry trends
- People's opinions

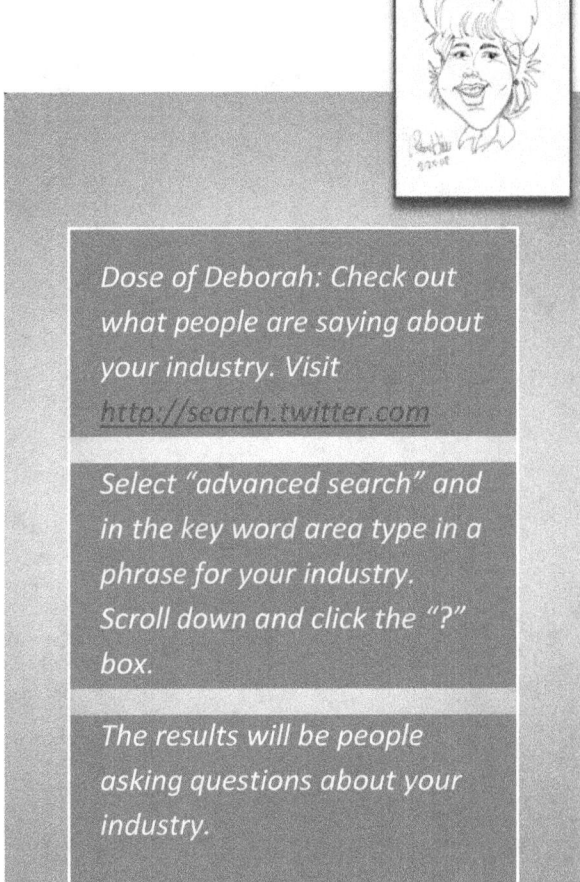

Twitter is such a great way of reaching out to people around the world and sharing opinions, asking questions, and having discussions. Of course, it is also a powerful tool for sharing company updates, video and images.

Dose of Deborah: Check out what people are saying about your industry. Visit http://search.twitter.com

To help get you started, I have created a daily to do list for how to use Twitter without just being someone who pushes out sales pitches. The key to Twitter is the interaction.

Select "advanced search" and in the key word area type in a phrase for your industry. Scroll down and click the "?" box.

I created a daily to do list that will allow you to be visible and involved without taking too much time. In fact, once you have this down to a science, you may decide to visit Twitter (through HootSuite) in the morning and at the end of the day. But first – just start once a day and see how it goes.

The results will be people asking questions about your industry.

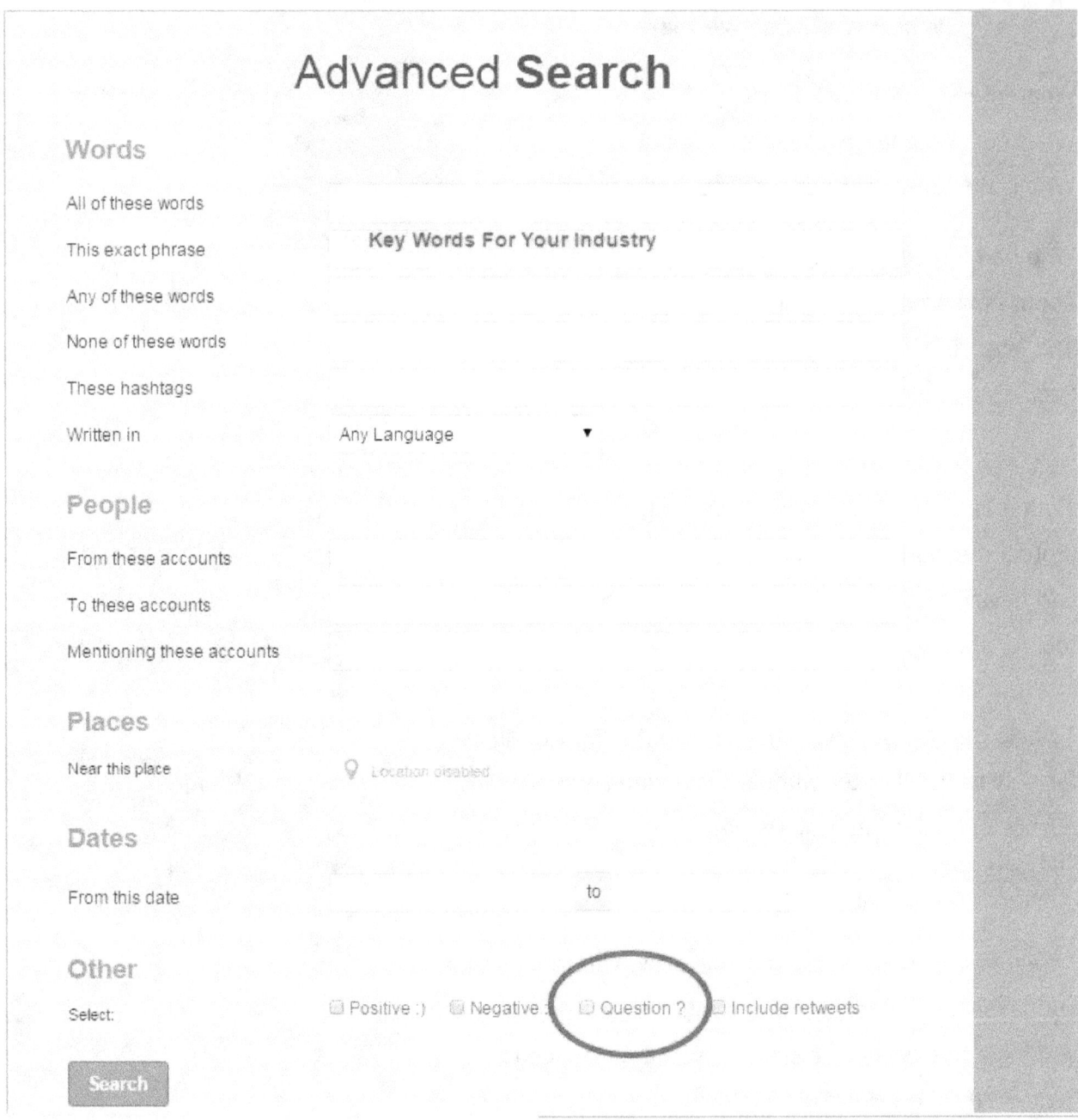

How to Create a Social Media Roadmap

Twitter To-Do List

✓	Item
☐	Sign into HootSuite
☐	Review "Mentions" and "Direct Messages" and respond
☐	Click on their name – if you are not following them…follow them
☐	Write a tweet about your business, quote, blog link, webpage, etc.
☐	Review your stream of keyword searches for news of value
☐	Retweet (edit) Add a comment in front of RT
☐	NOTE: Make sure you click on the link in the tweet you are sharing to ensure it is legitimate and of value.
☐	Repeat five times.
☐	Post an open ended question. (i.e. what is your biggest challenge today?)
☐	Write a tweet about your business
☐	**Friday:** Highlight those that mentioned you, retweeted your updates or followed you this week with #FF
☐	#FF stands for Follow Fridays

www.TheSocialMediaRoadmap.com
Copyright 2014

Instagram

Instagram is growing in popularity and is the social media vehicle to watch in 2015 and beyond.

Instagram is an app that you download onto your handheld device and then using the camera on your smart phone, you are able to upload images that you take to Instagram, Facebook, Twitter or other sites on the Internet.

The app allows you to easily edit the images, add filters, captions and comments to enhance the message you are sending. Like Twitter and Facebook, people follow you to see what images you will share.

This started as a way for people to share pictures of food, animals, and selfies, lots and lots of selfies, but businesses are starting to use this extremely popular app to connect with their audience.

From the Instagram business blog, here is an overview of the direction of this widely popular visual application:

We're proud to announce that there are now more than 300 million accounts on Instagram. Over the past four years, what began as two friends with a dream has grown into a global community that shares more than 70 million photos and videos each day.

For brands, this means that Instagram has a larger audience to engage and share beautiful and compelling imagery with — from Patagonia's shots of nature lovers in the wild to the way Disney's draws on its storytelling tradition to bring its characters to life through photos.

Today, we're also pleased to announce verified badges, which will make it easier for people to identify and follow the authentic brands they care about. When an account is verified, a blue badge will appear next to its name in its profile as well as in search. These badges will start rolling out in the coming days and will be assigned to public figures and brands that have a high chance of being impersonated.

Finally, as more people and businesses join, keeping Instagram authentic is critical. We're committed to doing everything possible to keep Instagram free from the fake and spammy accounts that plague many of the growing communities on the web, and that's why we're finishing up some important work that began earlier this year.

If you have a Facebook account, Instagram, a subsidiary of the behemoth social media site, you are able to connect and invite your Facebook friends and followers to see the images you post on Instagram.

Take advantage of the visual aspect of this app to invite followers to share their best photos using your products, tasting your food, visiting your location.

You can also upload video to Instagram, insert #hashtag phrases to assist with being found.

Visit some of the larger brands already embracing Instagram and take a page from their marketing book. See what they are doing and see how that might work for your business. We are all just trying different things to see what works; there isn't a right or wrong way, so jump in with both feet and give it a try.

The thing I like about Instagram is the fact that you use the app with your phone so you can be "in the moment," real-time with your followers.

As with all of the other social sites – make sure that you recognize, acknowledge and respond to those engaging with your photos. If someone makes a comment; say thank you, ask for more information – and "like" them back. It is all about building those relationships!

Brand using Instagram:

- **American Express**
- **Nordstrom**
- **Ann Taylor**
- **Jet Blue**
- **Disneyland**
- **Intel**
- **Virgin America**
- **Taco Bell**
- **LA Clippers**
- **NFL**

Left blank for your notes

Section Three: Create Your Unique Roadmap

It is time to get started. Narrow the field:

Must Have NOW: what do you need to start with first. Select one or two areas of marketing that you have started and wish to expand, believe is the most important or started and abandoned and want to start over. On a piece of paper, list what that one thing is.

- Monthly newsletter
- Weekly blog
- Daily Facebook or Twitter
- Better LinkedIn participation

Short Term Goals: what do you need to make it happen? Do you need additional training, technical support, content help? Now list what you need to bring that goal to life. Assign the name(s) of the person responsible, the help you need, the money that needs to be allocated and finally select a date for when you will begin.

Long Term Goals: On a separate page, write out the additional components you would like to add to your Social Media Roadmap. For example, you are starting with a monthly newsletter, perhaps in three months you want to add a blog and three months later you want to give Twitter a try.

How to Create a Social Media Roadmap

Time Commitment: Daily/Weekly/Monthly

Understand going into the process that your biggest expense will be time. So how much time are you willing to dedicate?

When will you be active – first thing in the morning? At lunch? At the end of the day?

Once you have determined this for your schedule; put it on the calendar. If you are going to dedicated the first hour of the day to writing, reading, listening, responding and research, then make sure it becomes a standing calendar entry.

Resources Needed

Identify what you will need to start and to continue your participation.

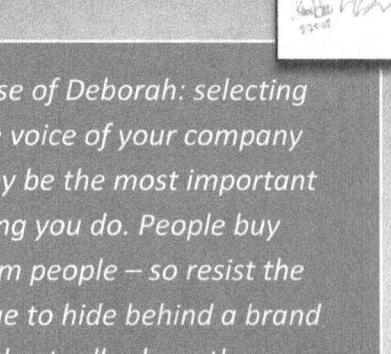

- Initial technical support – who will provide?
- Initial training – who will provide?
- Creation of an editorial calendar – where will the updates come from, who will write?
- Content writers – determine guest writers that can also contribute, who are they and how often will they provide content?
- Set a monthly budget for additional Facebook and Twitter advertisements.
- Determine who will review the participation and activity each month.
- List where the images and video will come from ; will you take the photos, will marketing provide, will you purchase online images, will you hire a photographer?

Dose of Deborah: selecting the voice of your company may be the most important thing you do. People buy from people – so resist the urge to hide behind a brand and actually share the name of the person doing the writing – whether it is the President, a PR person, a marketing person or someone from options – give the public a name.

Corporate Voice

Finally – what is your corporate voice? Will you use humor? Big words? Sarcasm (remember this is difficult to convey in writing) Best practices? Is the voice from the President or an entry level employee or a marketing executive? Who will be the voice/face of your company?

My Social Media Roadmap Worksheets

It is time to put your plan in writing. Starting with your most immediate goals, what do you need to start on this afternoon?

Vehicle: this is the tactic you need to work on; your website, your LinkedIn profile, coming up with an editorial calendar, creating a Facebook page, etc. Keep your goals simple – don't try to take on too much to start or you will immediately feel overwhelmed. There are only three spots here for a reason.

Time table: When do you plan to complete – put a date in this box. If the date comes and goes without completion, don't panic, don't give up – just put in a new date.

Frequency: Once this goal is up and running, how frequently do you plan to participate? If it is Facebook or LinkedIn – daily is probably a conservative time frame. If it is Twitter – more than once a day will be necessary.

Needs: what do you need to work on, complete and then sustain this goal? Do you need training? A web developer? A content writer? Software? A computer?

Responsibility: who will execute this project and who will sustain it? The responsibility may be shared. For example you may outsource the creation and the training and then bring the ongoing participation in house. But someone needs to own this – who will it be?

Immediate Goals

Vehicle	Time Table	Frequency	Needs	Responsibility

Focusing on the Future

Now that you have determined your most immediate goals, what will you work on next?

Will you create a series of e-books? Start a newsletter or a blog? Will you begin a video series?

Using the instructions from the Immediate Goals, complete the next two sections.

- For short term think 6-12 months.
- For Long Term, one year and beyond.

How to Create a Social Media Roadmap

Short Term Goals

Vehicle	Time Table	Frequency	Needs	Responsibility

Long Term Goals

Vehicle	Time Table	Frequency	Needs	Responsibility

Quick Summary — 6 Tips for Creating an Effective Social Media Roadmap

1. Create a plan.

    Determine your goal:

    - Connect with Customers
    - Drive traffic to your website
    - Brand awareness
    - Organic search engine optimization

    Determine your audience

    - B2B
    - B2C
    - Age/Gender/Economic and Educational level

2. Select the best vehicles to combine the goal with the audience

    Use the best resource for your business.

    - LinkedIn and blogging are best for brand recognition and business conversations
    - Pinterest, Instagram and blogging best for visual products and services
    - YouTube effective for manufacturing, instructional and retail businesses
    - Facebook is great for building a younger community of shoppers
    - Twitter is best for real time conversation

3. Measure effectiveness. Use online tools such as
    - Klout.com
    - Facebook Pages Reach
    - Google page rank
    - Alexa website ranking tool
    - OnlineIDCalculator.com

4. Timing is everything.
    - Be consistent
    - Tuesday/Wednesday/Thursday are most popular days for participation
    - Lunch time is when posts are read most frequently
    - Weekends your participation will stand out from the competition
    - Eastern standard time most widely used

How to Create a Social Media Roadmap

5. Social = 2-way conversation.

   Listen and respond

   - Google Alerts
   - Twitter Searches
   - Yelp
   - Angie's List
   - Ask questions
   - Poll on Facebook or LinkedIn
   - Invite conversation on your blog
   - Host a radio show, offer a podcast or webinar where guests can call in with questions
   - Special offers.
   - Create special offers for online communities
   - LinkedIn company page – create an "special offer" page
   - Schedule customer appreciation coupons or special offers

   Dose of Deborah: Effective social media roadmaps focus on the development of relationships rather than the opportunity to sell. People buy from those they know, like and trust and social media allows you the opportunity to fully engage with your prospects.

   Utilize check-in sites.

   - Check-in sites are used for retailers, restaurant and destination locations. Great for building in person community:
   - Four Square
   - Facebook Places

6. Integrate social media.
   - Make it easy for visitors to travel between your website and your social media sites and vice versa.
   - Include badges from your blog, website, e-newsletter and press releases to your company Facebook page, LinkedIn profile, Twitter account, YouTube channel and Pinterest Boards.
   - Include links to your social media accounts in the signature line of your emails.
   - Include your social media information on your business cards.
   - Include a full hyperlink of your website from the profile pages and image/video descriptions, make sure you include http://
   - Use geographical terms in all of your online content so that your organic search results are more effective for customers seeking your business within their community, county or state.

One Final Word on the Subject

Change is coming. Social media is now a given. Consumers expect to be able to communicate with a brand via social media and if they are not available or responsive, they will move on to a competitor that is.

I've been doing a little research, listening and reading what the experts have to say and following are my tips based on my own experience and research.

The days of FREE are over. If you have a Facebook company page, you've already realized that unless you allocate advertising dollars to boost a post or your page, those that "like" your page are not seeing your updates unless they seek you out. So if you intend to continue with Facebook – expect to put your money where your participation is.

Twitter isn't far behind. This incredibly powerful "real-time" venue has gotten so cluttered with automated messages and partial conversations that if you want to be visible, you'll need to consider advertising. However, even without a budget, this is still one of my favorite places to hang out – more later.

On 12-13-14 I was asked to give a presentation on trends for 2015 and as part of that process I created a 2015 Internet Participation Decision Roadmap.
In that presentation I listed the five key areas of focus for 2015 – in my opinion:

1. **Listen:** 5 out of 6 consumer comments on social media go unanswered. Be a great listener and also respond in a timely manner. People want to know they can connect with someone with a company they do business with – it will help you to stand out from the noise.

2. **Original Content:** Content is still the number one way to share your knowledge and keep your name in front of your prospects. Create an editorial calendar and stick to it! Check out my paperback How to Create Your Editorial Calendar for Press Releases, Newsletters and Articles.

How to Create a Social Media Roadmap

3. **Images/Video:** By 2017 2/3s of all searches will be via YouTube. Use simple tools like Animoto to create videos of your products. Use video capture on your Google Hangouts and upload or create a short Vine video using gif software. (check out www.imgfip.com).

4. **Mobile:** More people use their hand held device to search, share and shop. What does your website/blog look like on a Smart Phone or a tablet? Is it user friendly? Look into other ways to stand out in the mobile world. Consider creating an app. Check out [CampTech](#) for assistance.

5. **You!** This is the biggest message of all. People do business with people, not companies. So stop hiding in social media behind your company name. Consumers want to hear what the leaders of companies have to say. Consider signing all of your tweets with a hashtag of your initials. It lets people know there is a real person behind the comments.

Remember that the key word in social media is SOCIAL. That means being available and responsive, asking questions, listening, sharing your thoughts and opinions. Be authentic, that is what will help set you apart from the competition and be visible to your target prospects.

The most important thing to remember is that you need to do SOMETHING to keep your name in front of prospects so that when they are in the need for your products or services, they will remember you.

Customers buy from those they like and trust and social media provides the perfect opportunity to engage with our customers even before we meet. However, to be effective you need a plan.

You don't have to do it alone. Consider hiring an experienced web writer to assist with creating and executing your content plan. At AllWrite Ink, our writers will meet with your team to create a plan and then do the research, the writing and the uploading to the Internet to ensure you stay on schedule. Give us a call to learn more. 330-414-8792.

Or visit www.TheSocialMediaRoadmap.com.

Happy Travels! Deborah Chaddock Brown

Deborah@allwriteink.com

About the Author

Deborah Chaddock Brown is the founder of AllWrite Ink, an Internet writing firm specializing in helping companies build customer relationships through their website and social media presence. Deborah is a trainer, speaker and published author.

Connect with her directly: deborah@allwriteink.com

Deborah is the author of:

How to Create an Editorial Calendar

How to Promote Your Event with Social Media – an e-workbook

It's a Party: Planning a Successful Retail Sales Event

Back to Basics: 30 tips to market your small business and establish your expert status in the industry

Policy for Social Media Manual - 16 policies and procedures to assist companies with defining acceptable social media behavior on and off the job.

Contributing author in:

49 Marketing Secrets that work to grow sales,

Age of Conversation, Volume 2

Age of Conversation, Volume 3

Best Kept Marketing Secrets

You can follow me on http://twitter.com/thesmroadmap

Visit my Linked In Page. For more information about AllWrite Ink.

To hire Deborah Chaddock Brown as a speaker or to facilitate a Social Media training session.

www.ingramcontent.com/pod-product-compliance
Lightning Source LLC
Chambersburg PA
CBHW081612200526
45167CB00019B/2907